WHO IS GOD?

An Essential Guide To Understanding God's Nature And His Purpose For Your Life

OLABODE WINSALA

SOPHOS BOOKS

Who is God?

Published by
Sophos Books
Croydon
UK
sophosbooks.com

Unless otherwise stated, all Scripture quotations are taken from The Authorised *King James Version* of the Bible.

ISBN 978-1-905669-17-2

Cover design by *Tope Enoch*
Printed in the United Kingdom

CONTENTS

To my children, Tobi, the leader of the pack, David, the beginning of my strength, Mary-Elizabeth, our Princess, the evidence of our deliverance and God's intervention, Nathan, the gifted one, and Daniel, our prayer.
To Tai and Kenny Odelusi and EniOluwa Adegbulu, my children Godward.

ACKNOWLEDGEMENTS

First and foremost, I give all glory and honour to God, who entrusted this work into my hands and guided me through every step of the journey. Without His grace and direction, none of this would have been possible.

I also want to extend my deepest appreciation to everyone I have encountered on my life's journey so far, each of whom has contributed to this work in ways both direct and indirect. To my fellow labourers at *The Disciples and Men Arise* fellowships; your shared experiences, support, and prayers have been an inspiration. The teachings and fellowship at *Lea Valley Church*, Waltham Abbey, have been invaluable in shaping both my faith and this work.

A heartfelt thanks to my good friends and accomplished writers, Dr. Stoney Adegbulu and Kayode Kamson; for your invaluable encouragement, thought-provoking discussions, and gentle-yet-firm push when I needed it most. Bishop Fredrick Okhimamhe, thank you for your insightful words of encouragement and helpful hints that have guided me along the way. Florence Adewuyi, I am deeply grateful for your timely outreach and unwavering support.

I also wish to thank Umit and Gulcan Genc, my colleagues at work, with whom I have shared countless individual sessions over the years. Your constant curiosity, keen interest, and listening ears have been instrumental in planting the seed that grew into this work.

To Pastor Tokunbo Obasa, your prophetic prayers and words of encouragement have been a source of strength, for which I am deeply thankful. My brother, Dipo Winsala, thank you for always being there for me, providing steadfast support and encouragement.

Above all, to my wife, Tokunbo, my priceless treasure, your relentless prayers and unwavering support have been the backbone of this work. I am endlessly grateful to God for the gift of you in my life. To my children, whose constant prayers and love have lifted me up time and time again, I am truly blessed beyond measure to have such gifts as these from God.

Finally, to every reader of this work, thank you. You make the journey worthwhile, and for that, I am immensely grateful.

INTRODUCTION

The key to understanding life itself begins with understanding who God is. This book, *Who is God?*, offers an essential exploration of God's nature, character, and purpose as revealed in Scripture. Whether you are a new believer or someone seeking deeper insight into the Christian faith, this book will help you build a solid foundation in your understanding of God.

However, it is important to remember that God is infinitely greater than anything we can fully comprehend or describe. As John 21:25 says of Jesus' works: "*And there are also many other things which Jesus did, the which, if they should be written every one, I suppose that even the world itself could not contain the books that should be written.*" Similarly, no book can exhaust the vastness of who God is.

This book is intended to whet your appetite—to **introduce you** to some of the essential truths about God and point you toward knowing Him more personally. It's a starting point in a lifelong journey of growing in your understanding of God through Scripture, prayer, and a relationship with Him.

As we journey through the Bible, we will uncover how God reveals Himself, His plan for humanity, and how His Word serves as both a **formal authority** and a **personal guide** for living a righteous and fulfilled life.

Throughout Scripture, God progressively reveals His nature through His **Name Jehovah**—like Jehovah Jireh (the Provider), Jehovah Rapha (the Healer), and Jehovah Shalom (the God of Peace)—and through His actions as Creator, Sustainer, Redeemer, and Judge. This book will delve into these aspects of God's identity, showing how they impact our daily lives.

One crucial theme explored in this book is the **power and authority of God's Word**. The Bible serves as both the **written Word**—a permanent record of God's statutes, commandments, and promises—and as a **procedural manual** for life. It also stands as God's binding legal framework, instructing us in righteousness, warning of judgment, and pointing to redemption through Jesus Christ.

In this book, you will also find personal testimonies that highlight how God works in real-life situations—providing healing, guidance, and transformation in the lives of His people. These stories bring practical insight into the way God actively engages with His creation today.

From understanding God's eternal nature, to knowing Him as Father, to experiencing the transforming power of the Holy Spirit and His Kingdom, this book will guide you into a deeper relationship with the One who holds the answers to life's most important questions.

1

GOD IN ETERNITY PAST

The Concept of God Existing Before Time

The concept of eternity is difficult for the human mind to grasp. It implies an existence without beginning or end, transcending the limits of time and space. The Bible presents God as eternal, existing before the creation of the world and time itself. This idea is central to understanding God's nature and His relationship with His creation.

In Psalm 90:2, Moses declares, "*Before the mountains were brought forth, or ever Thou hadst formed the earth and the world, even from everlasting to everlasting, Thou art God.*" This verse highlights the eternal nature of God, emphasising that He existed long before the physical universe came into being. God's existence is not bound by time; He is the Creator of time and exists beyond its confines.

Biblical References to God's Eternal Nature

There are numerous scriptures that affirm God's eternal existence. In Genesis 1:1, we read, "*In the beginning, God created the heaven and the earth.*" The phrase "in the beginning" signifies the start of time, yet God was already present, indicating His existence outside of time.

Isaiah 57:15 describes God as "*the high and lofty One that inhabiteth eternity,*" underscoring His timeless nature. Revelation 1:8 records God's declaration, "*I AM ALPHA AND OMEGA, THE BEGINNING AND THE ENDING, WHICH IS, AND WHICH WAS, AND WHICH IS TO COME, THE ALMIGHTY,*" which further illustrates His eternal presence.

In the New Testament, John 1:1-3 speaks of the Word (Jesus Christ) existing with God from the begin -ing: "In the beginning was the Word, and the Word was with God, and the Word was God. The same was in the beginning with God. All things were made by Him; and without Him was not any thing made that was made." This passage reinforces the concept of God's eternal nature and His involvement in creation.

God Establishing Order in the Universe

Isaiah 43:10-11 provides profound insight into God's unique position and His role in establishing order in the universe. The passage states, "*Ye are My witnesses,*" *saith the LORD, "and My servant whom I have chosen, that ye may know and believe Me, and understand that I am*

He: Before Me there was no god formed, neither shall there be after Me. I, even I, am the LORD; and beside Me there is no saviour."

This declaration emphasises that God is the one true deity, with no equals or predecessors. It alludes to His sovereign authority in taking control of the universe, building His Kingdom, and bringing order to what was once a disorderly realm. This assertion of His unique divinity and ultimate sovereignty reinforces the understanding of His eternal nature and His unparalleled power.

God's act of creation was not merely the formation of physical matter but also the establishment of order and purpose. From the chaos and void, God brought forth a structured, harmonious universe, reflecting His wisdom and authority. This divine ordering is a testament to His sovereignty and His ability to bring order out of chaos.

The Significance of God's Eternal Existence for Believers

Understanding God's eternal nature has profound implications for believers. It assures us of His unchanging character, faithfulness, and sovereignty. Since God is eternal, He is not subject to the limitations and changes that affect the created world. This means His promises are reliable and His purposes are steadfast.

God's eternal existence also provides a foundation for our faith. Knowing that God transcends time and has always been present gives us confidence in His ability to fulfil His plans for humanity. It assures us that the same God who worked in the lives of biblical figures is active in our lives today.

Moreover, God's eternity offers comfort and hope. In a world where everything is temporary and uncertain, the eternal God remains a constant source of stability and assurance. As believers, we can trust that our relationship with God is secure and everlasting, anchored in His eternal nature.

Reflection and Application

Reflecting on God's eternal nature encourages us to deepen our trust in Him. We can meditate on scriptures that highlight His timeless existence and consider how this aspect of His character impacts our daily lives. In moments of uncertainty, recalling God's eternal presence can bring peace and reassurance.

In practical terms, we can apply this understanding by fostering a sense of awe and reverence for God. Recognising His eternal nature prompts us to worship Him with greater devotion and gratitude. It also inspires us to live with an eternal perspective, focusing on things that have lasting value rather than temporary concerns.

As we continue this journey of exploring who God is, let us hold firmly to the truth of His eternal existence. This foundational aspect of His character sets the stage for understanding His interactions with humanity and His divine purposes throughout history and into the future.

2

THE NAME OF GOD

The Power and Safety in the Name of God

Throughout the Bible, God's name represents His character, authority, and presence. Calling upon His name is an invitation to experience His power and protection. Proverbs 18:10 reminds us, "*The name of the LORD is a strong tower: the righteous runneth into it, and is safe.*" God's name is a place of refuge for His people, offering safety in times of trouble and comfort in times of need.

Calling Upon His Name

From the Old Testament to the New, we are encouraged to call upon the name of the LORD. Joel 2:32 promises, "*And it shall come to pass, that whosoever shall call on the name of the LORD shall be delivered.*" This deliverance speaks not only to physical protec-tion but also to spiritual salvation. God's name holds power over every circumstance, and He invites all to call on Him for provision, protection, healing, and deliverance.

The Name Jehovah

One of the most significant moments of divine revelation occurs in Exodus 6:2-3: "*And God spake unto Moses, and said unto him, I am the LORD: And I appeared unto Abraham, unto Isaac, and unto Jacob, by the name of God Almighty, but by my name JEHOVAH was I not known to them.*" This is the first instance where God introduces Himself as Jehovah, a name that encapsulates His eternal existence and covenant relationship with His people. Throughout the Old Testament, God continues to reveal aspects of His name that relate to His care for His people.

How God Wants to Be the God of Our Lives

Provision and Protection

God desires to be intimately involved in every aspect of our lives. He wants to provide for our needs, protect us from harm, and lead us on a path of righteousness. One of the many names of God is Jehovah Jireh, meaning "The LORD will provide." This name is introduced in Genesis 22:14 after God provides a ram for Abraham to sacrifice in place of Isaac: "*And Abraham called the name of that place Jehovah Jireh: as it is said to this day, In the mount of the LORD it shall be seen.*" This shows God's provision in moments of deep need and trust.

Another name is Jehovah Nissi, "*The LORD is my Banner.*" In Exodus 17:15, after a victorious battle, Moses builds an altar and names it "Jehovah Nissi."

God fights for His people, protecting them from enemies and shielding them from harm.

Healing and Deliverance

The name Jehovah Rapha means, "*The LORD who heals.*" In Exodus 15:26, God says to His people, "*I am the LORD that healeth thee.*" This name emphasises God's ability to heal not only physically but also emotionally and spiritually.

Sanctification and Redemption

God is also our sanctifier and redeemer. In Leviticus 20:8, God declares, "*And ye shall keep my statutes, and do them: I am the LORD which sanctify you.*" The name Jehovah Mkaddesh speaks to God's ongoing work of sanctification, setting us apart for His holy purposes.

Meeting Us at Every Crossroad

Throughout life, we encounter various challenges and crossroads where we need God's intervention. Whether in moments of weakness, sickness, or spiritual attack, God meets us where we are, revealing His name in powerful and personal ways. Through His name, we find deliverance, healing, peace, and guidance. Psalm 23:1 declares, "*The LORD is my shepherd; I shall not want.*" As our shepherd, He guides us through the valleys of life, providing exactly what we need in every season.

3

GOD PROVING HIS SUBJECTS

Examples of God Testing His People in the Bible

Throughout the Bible, God has tested His people to reveal their faith, obedience, and trust in Him. These tests are not meant to tempt or lead to failure but to refine and strengthen their character and faith. Let's explore some notable examples of how God proved His subjects.

1. Abraham and Isaac (Genesis 22:1-19)

One of the most profound tests in the Bible is when God commanded Abraham to sacrifice his beloved son Isaac. This test was designed to examine Abraham's faith and obedience. Despite the emotional and moral challenge, Abraham demonstrated his trust in God by preparing to sacrifice Isaac. At the last moment, God intervened, providing a ram as a substitute offering. This test not only confirmed Abraham's unwavering faith but also foreshadowed God's ultimate sacrifice of His own Son, Jesus Christ, for humanity's redemption.

2. Job's Suffering (Job 1-2,42)

Job is another powerful example of a faithful servant tested by God. Despite losing his wealth, children, and health, Job remained steadfast in his faith. His friends and even his wife urged him to curse God, but Job refused. Throughout his intense suffering, Job sought understanding and maintained his trust in God's justice and sovereignty. In the end, God restored Job's fortunes, rewarding his faithfulness and demonstrating that God's purposes often transcend human understanding.

3. The Israelites in the Wilderness (Exodus 15-17, Numbers 13-14)

After their miraculous deliverance from Egypt, the Israelites faced numerous tests in the wilderness. They encountered challenges such as lack of water, food, and opposition from enemies. These tests were meant to teach them dependence on God and trust in His provision. Unfortunately, the Israelites often failed these tests, grumbling and doubting God's care. However, through these experiences, God revealed His patience, mercy, and faithfulness, eventually leading a new generation into the Promised Land.

4. Gideon and the Midianites (Judges 6-7)

Gideon's story is an example of God testing and using an unlikely hero. Initially, Gideon doubted his ability to lead Israel against the Midianites. God patiently provided signs to confirm His call. When Gideon finally assembled an army, God reduced the number of soldiers from 32,000 to 300 to ensure that the victory would be attributed to divine intervention rather than human strength. This test of faith highlighted God's power and the importance of trusting in Him rather than relying on human resources.

Purpose and Outcomes of Tests

The tests that God administered had specific purposes and yielded significant outcomes.

1. Revealing Faith and Obedience:

Tests reveal the true nature of a person's faith and commitment to God. For instance, Abraham's willingness to sacrifice Isaac demonstrated his complete obedience and trust in God's promises.

2. Refining Character

Just as gold is refined by fire, tests serve to purify and strengthen believers' character. Job's trials, for example, deepened his understanding of God's sovereignty and justice, resulting in a more profound faith.

3. Teaching Dependence on God

Tests teach believers to rely on God rather than their own strength or resources. The Israelites' experiences in the wilderness were designed to cultivate trust in God's provision and guidance.

4. Demonstrating God's Power

Through tests, God's power and faithfulness are often displayed. Gideon's victory over the Midianites with a small army underscored that success comes from God's intervention, not human might.

5. Foreshadowing Greater Truths

Some tests foreshadow greater spiritual truths and events. Abraham's test with Isaac prefigured the sacrificial offering of Jesus Christ for the salvation of humanity.

Lessons for Believers Today

The tests faced by Biblical figures offer valuable lessons for believers today. As Paul said, *"Whatever things were written before were written for our learning"* (Romans 15:4). Some of the lessons we can derive include the following:

1. Trust in God's Sovereignty

Even in difficult and perplexing situations, believers are called to trust in God's sovereignty and wisdom. Like Job, we may not always understand the reasons behind our trials, but we can trust that God is in control.

2. Obedience and Faithfulness

Obedience to God's commands, even when they are challenging, is a mark of true faith. Abraham's example encourages us to follow God's will, trusting in His promises.

3. Dependence on God

Recognising our dependence on God is crucial. The Israelites' experiences remind us to seek God's guidance and provision in every aspect of our lives.

4. Strength through Trials

Trials and tests are opportunities for growth. They refine our character and deepen our relationship with God, as seen in the lives of Biblical figures like Gideon.

5. Hope in God's Faithfulness

The outcome of tests in the Bible often underscores God's faithfulness. Believers can find hope in knowing that God is faithful to His promises and will ultimately bring about His purposes.

Reflection and Application

Reflecting on the tests faced by Biblical figures encourages us to examine our own faith and obedience. We can draw strength from their examples and apply the lessons learned to our lives. In times of trial, we can trust in God's sovereignty, remain obedient to His commands, and depend on His provision.

In practical terms, we can cultivate a deeper trust in God by studying His Word, praying for wisdom and strength, and seeking fellowship with other believers. By doing so, we prepare ourselves to face the tests that may come our way, confident that God is with us and will use these experiences to refine and strengthen our faith.

As we continue exploring who God is, let us remember that He is a God who proves His subjects, not to cause them to stumble, but to reveal and strengthen their faith. Through these tests, we come to know Him more deeply and trust in His unwavering faithfulness.

4

GOD'S PERSONAL ACCOUNT OF CREATION AND THE FALL OF MAN

The Creation Story According to Genesis

The Bible begins with the majestic account of creation in Genesis 1, where God speaks the universe into existence. "*In the beginning, God created the heavens and the earth*" (Genesis 1:1). Over six days, God creates light, sky, land, seas, plants, celestial bodies, animals, and finally, humanity. Each act of creation is declared "good" by God, highlighting the perfection and intentionality of His work.

On the sixth day, God creates humans in His own image: "*So God created man in His own image, in the image of God created He him; male and female created He them*" (Genesis 1:27). This unique creation, made to reflect God's own nature, is given dominion over the earth and tasked with stewarding His creation.

The Fall of Man and Its Implications

Genesis 2 provides additional details about the create-ion of humans and the Garden of Eden, a paradise where Adam and Eve live in perfect harmony with God and creation. However, this harmony is disrupted in Genesis 3, where the serpent (identified later in the Bible as Satan) tempts Eve to eat from the tree of the knowledge of good and evil, which God had forbidden.

Eve, and subsequently Adam, eat the forbidden fruit, leading to the fall of man. This act of disobedience introduces sin into the world, bringing consequences such as pain, suffering, and death. God's response includes curses on the serpent, the ground, and the introduction of labour pains and mortality for humans. Despite this, God promises redemption through the "*seed of the woman*" (Genesis 3:15), fore-shadowing Jesus Christ.

Lucifer's Fall and Its Role in the Fall of Man

To fully understand the context of the fall, we must look at the origins of the serpent's rebellion against God. Isaiah 14:12-15 and Ezekiel 28:12-17 provide prophetic insights into Lucifer's fall from grace, which parallels the downfall of earthly kings but also alludes to the spiritual rebellion of Satan.

> "How art thou fallen from heaven, O Lucifer, son of the morning! How hast thou cut down to the ground, which did weaken the nations! For thou hast said in thine heart, 'I will ascend

> into heaven; I will exalt my throne above the stars of God; I will sit also upon the mount of the congregation, in the sides of the north: I will ascend above the heights of the clouds; I will be like the Most High.' Yet thou shalt be brought down to hell, to the sides of the pit."
>
> **Isaiah 14:12-15**

This passage highlights Lucifer's pride and desire to usurp God's throne, leading to his downfall.

> "Thou sealest up the sum, full of wisdom, and perfect in beauty. Thou hast been in Eden the garden of God; every precious stone was thy covering, the sardius, topaz, and the diamond, the beryl, the onyx, and the jasper, the sapphire, the emerald, and the carbuncle, and gold: the workmanship of thy tabrets and of thy pipes was prepared in thee in the day that thou wast created. Thou art the anointed cherub that covereth; and I have set thee so: thou wast upon the holy mountain of God; thou hast walked up and down in the midst of the stones of fire. Thou wast perfect in thy ways from the day that thou wast created, till iniquity was found in thee. By the multitude of thy merchandise they have filled the midst of thee with violence, and thou hast sinned: Therefore I will cast thee as profane out of the mountain of God: and I will destroy thee, O covering cherub, from the midst of the stones of fire. Thine heart was lifted up because of thy beauty, thou hast corrupted thy wisdom by reason of thy brightness: I will cast thee to the ground, I will lay thee before kings, that they may behold thee."
>
> **Ezekiel 28:12-17**

Ezekiel describes Lucifer's initial perfection and subsequent corruption due to pride and rebellion. His fall from God's favour and expulsion from heaven set the stage for his role in the Garden of Eden.

The Connection Between Lucifer's Fall and the Fall of Man

Lucifer's rebellion against God is characterized by pride and a desire to be equal to God. This same pride and deceit lead to his role as the serpent in the Garden of Eden. His temptation of Eve introduces doubt and desire for knowledge and power, echoing his own fall.

The serpent's words, "*Ye shall not surely die... For God doth know that in the day ye eat thereof, then your eyes shall be opened, and you shall be as gods, knowing good and evil" (Genesis 3:4-5),* mirror Lucifer's own ambitions. By succumbing to this temptation, Adam and Eve replicate Lucifer's rebellion, leading to their own downfall and the introduction of sin into humanity.

The Significance of These Events for Believers

Understanding Lucifer's fall and his role in the Garden of Eden provides believers with a deeper insight into the nature of sin and rebellion against God. It emphasises the destructive power of pride and the consequences of turning away from God's commands.

For believers, this narrative serves as a cautionary

tale about the subtlety of temptation and the importance of obedience to God. It also highlights God's sovereignty and the overarching plan for redemption through Jesus Christ, promised immediately after the fall.

Reflection and Application

Reflecting on the fall of Lucifer and the fall of man encourages believers to remain vigilant against pride and temptation. It reminds us of the need for humility, obedience, and reliance on God's wisdom rather than our own understanding.

In practical terms, we can apply these lessons by cultivating a heart of humility, seeking God's guidance through prayer and scripture, and being aware of the spiritual battle that continues in our lives. Understanding the origins of rebellion helps us recognise and resist the tactics of the enemy.

As we continue our exploration of who God is, recognising the spiritual context of creation and the fall underscores His holiness, justice, and the depth of His love in providing a means for redemption. This foundational understanding prepares us to appreciate the subsequent chapters on the Kingdom of God, God's plan for humanity and His attributes.

5

THE KINGDOM OF GOD

The Nature of God's Kingdom

The Kingdom of God is eternal, unshakable, and sovereign. Daniel 2:44 declares, "*And in the days of these kings shall the God of heaven set up a kingdom, which shall never be destroyed.*" God's Kingdom transcends earthly kingdoms and exists beyond time, extending both into the present and future.

Sovereignty and Eternal Reign

The sovereignty of God is central to His Kingdom. His reign is eternal, and no force can oppose or overthrow His rule. Psalm 145:13 affirms, "*Thy kingdom is an everlasting kingdom, and thy dominion endureth throughout all generations.*" God's authority and dominion encompass all creation.

The Culture and Essentials of His Kingdom

Righteousness, Peace, and Joy

The Kingdom of God is marked by righteousness, peace, and joy. Romans 14:17 tells us, "*For the kingdom of God is not meat and drink; but righteousness, and peace, and joy in the Holy Ghost.*" These three virtues define the life of a believer in God's Kingdom. Righteousness refers to right standing with God, peace speaks to the wholeness and calm that comes from His presence, and joy is the deep, abiding happiness that comes through the Holy Spirit.

Kingdom Values

The culture of God's Kingdom is countercultural to the world. In Matthew 5, the Sermon on the Mount provides a blueprint for Kingdom living, including the values of meekness, mercy, purity, and peacemaking. Micah 6:8 sums up these values: "*He hath shewed thee, O man, what is good; and what doth the LORD require of thee, but to do justly, and to love mercy, and to walk humbly with thy God?*"

Qualifications for His Kingdom

Who Can Enter the Kingdom?

Jesus clearly states in John 3:3, "*Except a man be born again, he cannot see the kingdom of God.*" The new birth—spiritual regeneration through faith in Christ—is the essential qualification for entering the Kingdom of God. It is not by works, status, or lineage, but by a transformed heart.

Repentance and Faith

Mark 1:15 records Jesus' call: "*The time is fulfilled, and the kingdom of God is at hand: repent ye, and believe the gospel.*" Repentance and faith are foundational to becoming part of the Kingdom. Without a heart change that turns from sin and believes in the good news of Christ, one cannot enter into this Kingdom.

The Way of the Kingdom

Living as Kingdom Citizens

As citizens of the Kingdom, believers are called to live in a way that reflects the nature and values of God's reign. Philippians 3:20 says, "*For our conversation is in heaven; from whence also we look for the Saviour, the Lord Jesus Christ.*" We are to represent God's Kingdom through our conduct, love, and faithfulness.

The Future of the Kingdom

The Kingdom of God will be fully realised when Christ returns to establish His reign in the new heavens and the new earth. The Scriptures describe this glorious future:

> "And I saw a new heaven and a new earth: for the first heaven and the first earth were passed away... And God shall wipe away all tears from their eyes; and there shall be no more death, neither sorrow, nor crying, neither shall there be any more pain: for the former things are passed away."
>
> **Revelation 21:1-4**

This eternal Kingdom is the hope of all believers, where righteousness will dwell, and God's presence will be fully manifest.

6

GOD'S PLAN FOR HUMANITY - THROUGH JESUS

The Promise of a Savior in the Old Testament

From the very moment sin entered the world through the disobedience of Adam and Eve, God set in motion a plan to redeem humanity. This plan is woven throughout the Old Testament, where various prophecies and promises point to the coming of a Savior.

The first gospel

After the fall, God pronounced judgment on the serpent and promised man's redemption through the "seed of the woman." He said, "*And I will put enmity between thee and the woman, and between thy seed and her seed; it shall bruise thy head, and thou shalt bruise his heel*" (Genesis 3:15). This *proto-evangelium,* or first gospel, foretells the ultimate victory of Jesus over Satan.

Abraham's Covenant

God's promise to Abraham in Genesis 12 "And in thee shall all families of the earth be blessed." is a significant part of this redemptive plan. This covenant establishes that through Abraham's lineage, the Saviour would come, bringing blessings to all nations.

Prophecies of the Messiah

The Old Testament is rich with prophecies about the coming Messiah. Isaiah 7:14 foretells the virgin birth: "*Therefore the LORD Himself shall give you a sign; Behold, a virgin shall conceive, and bear a Son, and shall call His name IMMANUEL.*" The Bible speaks of the Messiah's divine nature and eternal reign:

> "For unto us a child is born, unto us a son is given, and the government shall be on his shoulders. And his name shall be called Wonderful, Counselor, The Mighty God, The Everlasting Father, The Prince of Peace."
>
> **Isaiah 9:6-7**

Other significant prophecies include Micah 5:2, which predicts the Messiah's birthplace in Bethlehem, and Zechariah 9:9, which describes the Messiah's triumphant entry into Jerusalem on a donkey.

Jesus' Life, Death, and Resurrection

The New Testament reveals the fulfilment of these prophecies in the person of Jesus Christ. His life, death, and resurrection are the cornerstone of God's plan for humanity's redemption.

The Birth of Jesus

The Gospels of Matthew and Luke detail the miraculous birth of Jesus. Born of the Virgin Mary in Bethlehem, Jesus' birth fulfils the ancient prophecies and marks the incarnation of God as a human being. The angel's announcement to the shepherds declares the significance of His birth:

> "I bring you good tidings of great joy, which shall be to all people. For unto you is born this day in the city of David a Saviour, which is Christ the LORD."
>
> **Luke 2:10-11**

Jesus' Ministry

During His earthly ministry, Jesus demonstrated God's love, power, and authority. His Mission Statement was "Repent, for the Kingdom of God is nigh." He performed miracles, healed the sick, and taught with unparalleled wisdom. His teachings emphasised the Kingdom of God, calling people to repentance, faith, and a transformed life. Jesus' ministry also revealed His identity as the Son of God, fulfilling the messianic prophecies.

The Crucifixion

The climax of Jesus' mission was His sacrificial death on the cross. In fulfilment of Isaiah 53, which describes the suffering servant, Jesus willingly laid down His life to atone for humanity's sins. As He hung on the cross, He bore the weight of the world's sin, bridging the gap between a holy God and sinful humanity. His final words, "*It is finished*" (John 19:30), signify the completion of His redemptive work.

Jesus' Plea for Forgiveness

One of the most poignant moments during the crucifixion is Jesus' plea to the Father: "*Father, forgive them, for they know not what they do*" (Luke 23:34). This plea highlights Jesus' boundless mercy and compassion. Despite enduring immense suffering and injustice, Jesus intercedes for His persecutors, exemplifying the ultimate act of forgiveness. This moment underscores the depth of God's love and the extent of His grace, offering forgiveness even to those who participated in His crucifixion.

The Resurrection

Three days after His death, Jesus rose from the dead, conquering sin and death. The resurrection is the cornerstone of Christian faith, providing hope and assurance of eternal life. As Paul writes in 1 Corinthians 15:17, "*And if Christ be not raised, your faith is vain; ye are yet in your sins.*" The resurrection validates Jesus' divinity and the efficacy of His sacrifice.

The Significance of Jesus for Humanity's Redemption

Jesus' life, death, and resurrection have profound implications for humanity. Some of the undeniable impacts of His mission include the following:

1. Reconciliation with God

Through Jesus' sacrifice, believers are reconciled with God. As Paul states in Romans 5:10, "*For if, when we were enemies, we were reconciled to God by the death of his Son, much more, being reconciled, we shall be saved by His life!*" This reconciliation restores the broken relationship between humanity and God.

2. Forgiveness of Sins

Jesus' death provides the means for the forgiveness of sins. Ephesians 1:7 declares, "*In whom we have redemption through His blood, the forgiveness of sins, according to the riches of His grace.*" Believers are cleansed from their sins and set free from the bondage of sin.

3. Eternal Life

Jesus' resurrection ensures eternal life for all who believe in Him. John 3:16, one of the most well-known verses, affirms this promise: "*For God so loved the world, that He gave His only begotten Son, that WHOSOEVER believeth in Him should not perish, but have everlasting life.*" The resurrection guarantees that death is not the end for believers.

4. Adoption into God's Family

Through faith in Jesus, believers are adopted into God's family. Galatians 4:4-5 explains, "*But when the fulnesss of the time was come, God sent forth His Son, made of a woman, made under the law, to redeem them that were under the law, that we might receive adoption to sons.*" This adoption grants believers the status of children of God, with all the associated privileges.

5. Empowerment through the Holy Spirit

Jesus promised to send the Holy Spirit to empower and guide believers. Acts 1:8 records Jesus' promise: "*But ye shall receive power, after that the Holy Ghost is come upon you; and ye shall be witnesses unto Me in Jerusalem, and in all Judea, and in Samaria, and unto the uttermost part of the earth.*" The Holy Spirit equips believers to live godly lives and fulfil God's purposes.

Reflection and Application

Reflecting on God's plan for humanity through Jesus encourages believers to live in gratitude, faith, and obedience. Understanding the depth of God's love and the sacrifice of Jesus should inspire a response of worship and commitment. In practical terms, believers can apply these truths by:

- *Embracing the Gospel:* Fully accepting the good news of Jesus' life, death, and resurrection, and sharing it with others.

- *Living in Obedience:* Following Jesus' teachings and commandments, demonstrating love and faithfulness in everyday life.
- *Cultivating a Relationship with God:* Spending time in prayer, Bible study, and worship to grow closer to God.
- *Serving Others:* Reflecting Jesus' love by serving and caring for those in need.
- *Relying on the Holy Spirit:* Seeking the guidance and empowerment of the Holy Spirit in all aspects of life.

As we continue exploring who God is, recognising His plan for humanity through Jesus highlights His love, mercy, and desire for a restored relationship with His creation. This understanding lays a foundation for comprehending God's fatherhood, the role of the Holy Spirit, and His divine attributes.

7

GOD AS A FATHER

Biblical Depiction of God as a Father

The image of God as a Father is a central theme in the Bible, portraying a relationship that is both intimate and authoritative. This depiction emphasises God's care, guidance, discipline, and unconditional love for His children.

Old Testament References

In the Old Testament, God is often described as a Father to the nation of Israel. For instance, in Deuteronomy 32:6, Moses reminds the Israelites, "*Do ye thus requite the LORD, O foolish people and unwise? Is not He thy Father, that hath brought thee? Hath He not made thee, and established thee?*" This verse highlights God's role as both Creator and Father, underscoring His protective and nurturing nature.

God's intention to be Father to all nations and

peoples of the earth, starting from Israel is clear from His message to Pharaoh through Moses:

> "And thou shall say unto Pharaoh, "Thus saith the LORD. Israel is My son, even My firstborn: And I say unto thee, let My son go, that he may serve Me."
>
> **Exodus 4: 22-23**

In Isaiah 64:8, the prophet declares, "*But now, O LORD, Thou art our Father; We are the clay, and Thou art our potter; and we are all the work of Thy hand.*" This metaphor of God as a potter shaping the clay illustrates His hands-on involvement in the lives of His people, moulding them according to His will.

New Testament Revelation

The New Testament further reveals the fatherhood of God through the teachings of Jesus. In the Lord's Prayer, Jesus instructs His disciples to address God as "*Our Father in heaven*" (Matthew 6:9), signifying a personal and approachable relationship. Jesus frequently refers to God as His Father, emphasising their unique relationship and setting an example for believers to view God as their heavenly Father.

In the parable of the prodigal son (Luke 15:11-32), Jesus vividly portrays God's fatherly love. The father in the story represents God, who eagerly waits for the return of his wayward son and welcomes him back with open arms. This parable illustrates God's readiness to forgive and restore those who repent.

Attributes of God's Fatherhood

God's fatherhood encompasses several attributes that highlight His relationship with His children. Comprehending these attributes will enrich our rela -tionship with Him.

1. Love

God's love is central to His identity as a Father. In 1 John 3:1, we read, "*Behold, what manner of love the Father hath bestowed upon us, that we should be called the sons of God.*" And that is what we are! This love is unconditional, sacrificial, and everlasting, demonstrated supremely through the sending of His Son, Jesus Christ, for our redemption (John 3:16).

2. Discipline

As a loving Father, God also disciplines His children.

> "For whom the LORD loveth He chasteneth, and scourgeth every son whom He receiveth. If ye endure chastening, God dealeth with you as with sons; *for what one is he whom the father chasteneth not?*"
>
> **Hebrews 12:6-7**

God's discipline is not punitive but corrective, aimed at guiding believers towards holiness and righteousness.

3. Provision

God, as a Father, provides for the needs of His children. Jesus, in the sermon on the mount, reassured His followers,

> "Therefore take no thought, saying, what shall we eat? Or what shall we drink? Or wherewithal shall we be clothed?' For after all these things do the gentiles seek: For your heavenly Father knoweth that ye have need of all these things."
>
> **Matthew 6:31-32**

This promise underscores God's awareness and provision for our physical and spiritual needs.

4. Protection

God's fatherly protection is another vital aspect of His character. The psalmist declares,

> "The LORD is thy keeper: the LORD is thy shade upon thy right hand. The sun shall not smite thee by day, nor the moon by night. The LORD shall preserve thee from all evil: He shall preserve thy soul. The LORD shall preserve thy going out and thy coming in from this time forth, and even for evermore."
>
> **Psalm 121:5-8**

This assurance of protection reflects God's constant care and guardianship.

5. *Guidance*

As a Father, God provides guidance and wisdom to His children. God's word advises,

> "Trust in the LORD with all thine heart; and lean not on thine own understanding. In all thy ways acknowledge Him, and He shall direct thy paths."
>
> **Proverbs 3:5-6**

God's guidance is available to those who seek His direction and trust in His wisdom.

Approaching the Throne of Grace

One of the most comforting aspects of God's fatherhood is the invitation to approach Him confidently in times of need. Hebrews 4:16 encourages believers: "*Let us therefore come boldly unto the throne of grace, that we may obtain mercy, and find grace to help in time of need.*" This invitation reflects God's desire for His children to come to Him without fear, knowing that He is a compassionate and merciful Father.

The Role of Jesus

This access to God's throne is made possible through the finished work of Jesus on the cross. Jesus, our High Priest, has made a way for us to enter God's presence boldly. His sacrifice removes the barrier of sin, allowing us to approach God with confidence and receive His grace and mercy.

Receiving Grace and Mercy

Grace and mercy are essential aspects of God's fatherly care. Grace is the unmerited favour of God, freely given to us despite our unworthiness. Mercy is God's compassion in withholding the punishment we deserve. Together, they provide the foundation for our relationship with God, enabling us to live in His love and forgiveness.

The Dual Aspect of God's Nature

While God is our loving Father in this life, offering grace and mercy, He will also judge as the Almighty God in the life to come. This dual aspect of His nature is important to understand. As 2 Corinthians 5:10 states, "*For we must all appear before the judgment seat of Christ, that every one may receive the things done in his body, according to that he hath done, whether it be good or bad.*" This future judgment underscores the importance of living a life that honours God, knowing that we will one day give an account to Him.

How Believers Can Relate to God as Their Father

Understanding and embracing God as a Father transforms the believer's relationship with Him. Here are practical ways to relate to God as our Father:

1. Cultivating Trust and Dependence

Just as a child relies on their earthly father, believers are called to trust and depend on God for all aspects of their lives. This trust is built through prayer, studying Scripture, and experiencing God's faithfulness in daily life.

2. Accepting Discipline

Recognising God's discipline as an expression of His love helps believers to accept and learn from it. Hebrews 12:11 states, "*Now no chastening for the present seemeth to be joyous, but grievous: never-theless afterward it yieldeth the peaceable fruit of righteousness unto them which are exercised thereby.*"

3. Seeking His Provision

Believers can confidently approach God with their needs, knowing that He is a caring Father who provides. Philippians 4:19 promises, "*But my God shall supply all your need according to His riches in glory by Christ Jesus.*"

4. Resting in His Protection

Trusting in God's protection allows believers to live without fear. Psalm 46:1 declares, "God is our refuge and strength, a very present help in trouble."

5. Following His Guidance

Seeking God's will and following His guidance involves submitting to His wisdom and direction. This can be done through prayer, meditation on His Word, and seeking counsel from mature believers.

Reflection and Application

Reflecting on God as a Father encourages believers to deepen their relationship with Him. It reminds us of His constant presence, love, and care. This understanding should inspire us to live as His children, reflecting His character in our interactions with others.

In practical terms, believers can:

- *Engage in Regular Prayer:* Foster a conversational relationship with God, sharing your heart and seeking His guidance.
- *Study Scripture:* Delve into the Bible to understand more about God's fatherly attributes and His promises to His children.
- *Participate in Community:* Engage with other believers in fellowship, learning from one another and growing together in faith.
- *Serve Others:* Reflect God's love and care by serving those in need, demonstrating His fatherly compassion.
- *Cultivate Gratitude:* Regularly thank God for His provision, protection, discipline, and guid-

ance, recognising His fatherly role in your life.

As we continue exploring who God is, recognising Him as a Father enriches our understanding of His nature and deepens our relationship with Him. This foundation prepares us to explore the role of the Holy Spirit, the nature of God's divine attributes, and His work in the world.

8

THE NATURE AND ATTRIBUTES OF THE HOLY SPIRIT

The Person of the Holy Spirit

The Holy Spirit is the third person of the Trinity, co-equal with God the Father and God the Son. Understanding the Holy Spirit's role and nature is essential for a complete understanding of who God is.

The Holy Spirit in the Old Testament: In the Old Testament, the Holy Spirit is often referred to as the Spirit of God. The Spirit was active in creation, as seen in Genesis 1:2 "*And the earth was without form, and void; and darkness was upon the face of the deep. And the Spirit of God moved upon the face of the waters.*" The Spirit also empowered individuals for specific tasks, such as Bezalel, who was filled with the Spirit of God to craft the Tabernacle (Exodus 31:3).

The Holy Spirit in the New Testament: In the New Testament, the Holy Spirit's role becomes more prominent. Jesus promised the coming of the Holy Spirit, referring to Him as the Comforter or Helper. John

14:16-17 records Jesus' words: "*And I will pray the Father, and He shall give you another comforter that He may abide with you forever – Even the Spirit of truth.*"

On the day of Pentecost, the Holy Spirit descended upon the disciples, empowering them to preach the gospel and perform miracles (Acts 2). The Holy Spirit's indwelling presence in believers marks the new covenant relationship between God and His people.

The Role of the Holy Spirit in the Believer's Life

The Holy Spirit plays several crucial roles in the life of a believer. Some of these roles include the following:

1. Conviction of Sin

The Holy Spirit convicts individuals of their sin, leading them to repentance. John 16:8 explains, "*And when He is come, He will reprove the world of sin, and of righteousness, and of judgment.*"

2. Regeneration

The Holy Spirit is responsible for the new birth, regenerating believers and making them new creations in Christ. Titus 3:5 states, "*Not by works of righteousness which we have done, but according to His mercy He saved us, by the washing of regeneration, and renewing of the Holy Ghost.*"

3. Indwelling Presence

The Holy Spirit resides within believers, making them temples of God. 1 Corinthians 6:19-20 affirms, "*What? Know ye not that your body is the Temple of the Holy Ghost which is in you, which ye have of God, and ye are not your own? For ye are bought with a price: therefore, glorify God in your body, and in your spirit, which are God's.*"

4. Guidance and Teaching

The Holy Spirit guides believers into all truth and teaches them God's ways. John 14:26 says, "*But the Comforter, which is the Holy Ghost, whom the Father will send in My Name, He shall teach you all things, and bring all things to your remembrance whatsoever I have said unto you.*"

5. Empowerment

The Holy Spirit empowers believers for kingdom service and being a witness for Christ. Acts 1:8 records Jesus' promise, "*But ye shall receive power, after the Holy Ghost is come upon you: and ye shall be witnesses unto Me both in Jerusalem, and in all Judea, and in Samaria, and unto the uttermost part of the earth.*"

6. Sanctification

The Holy Spirit works in believers to sanctify them, transforming them into the image of Christ. 2 Corinthians 3:18 explains, "*But we all, with open face beholding as in a glass the glory of the LORD, are changed into the same image from glory to glory, even as by the Spirit of the LORD'"*

7. Help in Prayer

The Holy Spirit assists believers in prayer, especially when they are unsure of how to pray or what to pray about.

> "Likewise the Spirit also helpeth our infirmities: for we know not what we should pray for as we ought: but the Spirit itself maketh intercession for us with groanings which cannot be uttered. And He that searcheth the hearts knoweth what is the mind of the Spirit, because He maketh intercession for the saints according to the will of God."
>
> **Romans 8:26-27**

8. Giver of Spiritual Gifts

The Holy Spirit bestows spiritual gifts upon believers for the edification of the church. These gifts include speaking in tongues, prophecy, healing, miracles, and more. Paul describes these gifts in his epistle to the Corinthians:

> "Now there are diversities of gifts, but the same Spirit. And there are differences of administrations, but the same LORD. And there are diversities of operations, but it is the same God which worketh all in all. But the manifestation of the Spirit is given to every man to profit withal. For

to one is given by the Spirit the word of wisdom; to another the word of knowledge by the same Spirit; To another faith by the same Spirit; to another the gifts of healing by the same Spirit; To another the working of miracles; to another prophecy; to another discerning of spirits; to another divers kinds of tongues; to another the interpretation of tongues: But all these worketh that one and the selfsame Spirit, dividing to every man severally as He will."

I Corinthians 12:4-11

Attributes of God: Omniscience, Omnipotence, Omnipresence, and More

God possesses several divine attributes that define His nature and distinguish Him from His creation. These attributes are essential for understanding who God is.

1. *Omniscience*

God is all-knowing, possessing complete and perfect knowledge. Psalm 147:5 declares, "*Great is our LORD and of great power: His understanding is infinite.*" God's omniscience means He knows everything about the past, present, and future, as well as the thoughts and intentions of every heart.

2. *Omnipotence*

God is all-powerful, able to accomplish anything according to His will. Jeremiah 32:17 exclaims, "*Ah,*

LORD GOD! Behold, Thou hast made the heaven and the earth by Thy great power and stretched out arm, and there is nothing too hard for Thee." God's omnipotence is evident in His creation, miracles, and ultimate authority over all things.

3. *Omnipresence*

God is always present everywhere. This is how David expressed this truth:

> "Whither shall I go from Thy Spirit? Or Whither shall I flee from Thy presence? If I go up to the heavens, you are there; if I make my bed in the depths, you are there. If I ascend up into heaven, Thou art there: If I make my bed in hell, behold, Thou art there. If I take the wings of the morning, and dwell in the uttermost parts of the sea; Even there shall Thy hand lead me, and Thy right hand shall hold me." God's omnipresence assures believers that He is always with them, no matter where they are.
>
> **Psalm 139:7-10**

4. *Immutability*

God is unchanging in His nature, character, and promises. James 1:17 states, "*Every good gift and every perfect gift is from above, and cometh down from the Father of lights, with whom is no variableness, neither shadow of turning.*" God's immutability provides stability and assurance, as His love, faithfulness, and purposes remain constant.

5. Holiness

God is perfectly holy, completely separate from sin and morally pure. Isaiah 6:3 describes the seraphim calling out, "*Holy, holy, holy is the LORD of Hosts: the whole earth is full of His glory.*" God's holiness is the standard for His people, calling them to live holy lives.

6. Love

God is love, and His nature is defined by His selfless, sacrificial love. 1 John 4:8 declares, "*He that loveth not knoweth not God; for God is love.*" God's love is demonstrated supremely through the sending of His Son, Jesus Christ, to redeem humanity.

7. Justice

God is just and righteous in all His ways. Deuteronomy 32:4 affirms, "*He is the Rock, His work is perfect: for all His ways are judgment. A God of truth and without iniquity, just and right is He.*" God's justice ensures that He will judge sin and uphold righteousness.

Reflection and Application

Understanding the Holy Spirit and God's divine attributes will enrich our relationship with Him and inform our daily lives. Believers can:

- *Seek the Holy Spirit's Guidance:* Regularly pray

for the Holy Spirit's guidance and teaching, relying on His wisdom and direction.

- *Embrace God's Attributes:* Reflect on God's attributes and how they impact your understanding of Him. For example, trust in His omniscience and omnipotence in times of uncertainty.
- *Live in Holiness:* Strive to live a holy life, reflecting God's holiness in your thoughts, words, and actions.
- *Rest in God's Love:* Embrace God's love and allow it to transform your relationships and interactions with others.
- *Trust in God's Justice:* Have confidence that God will ultimately judge with fairness and righteousness and seek to promote justice in your own sphere of influence.

As we continue exploring who God is, understanding the Holy Spirit's role and God's divine attributes deepens our appreciation of His nature and work in our lives. This foundation prepares us to explore God's word, His various roles, His works, and His moral authority as the ultimate object of worship and devotion.

9

THE POWER AND AUTHORITY OF GOD'S WORD

The Nature of God's Word

God communicates in two primary ways: through His written Word, the Bible, and His spoken Word. The written Word is God's eternal, unchanging revelation, while the spoken Word refers to His direct communication, often prophetic, throughout history. Both forms work together to reveal God's heart and will.

God's Written Word

The Bible is the inspired Word of God, given to teach, correct, and instruct us in righteousness. As Paul states,

> "All scripture is given by inspiration of God, and is profitable for doctrine, for reproof, for correction, for instruction in righteousness: That the man of God may be perfect, thoroughly furnished unto all good works."
>
> **2 Timothy 3:16-17**

God's Spoken Word

The spoken Word often came through prophets or directly from God, such as in the creation narrative where God said, "*Let there be light*" (Genesis 1:3). Today, the Holy Spirit may speak to believers in line with God's written Word, providing personal guidance.

God's Word: The Act, Procedure, and Manual of Life

1. The Bible as the Act of Life

The Bible serves as the formal and binding authority of God over all creation. It contains His laws, ordinances, statutes, judgments, and resolutions. Through it, God establishes His divine authority over human life, providing a legal and moral framework that directs how individuals should live.

> "The law of the LORD is perfect, converting the soul: the testimony of the LORD is sure, making wise the simple. The statutes of the LORD are right, rejoicing the heart: the commandment of the LORD is pure, enlightening the eyes."
>
> **Psalm 19:7-9**

God's Authority and Court

The Bible reveals God as the ultimate Judge who rules over the universe. His laws are not merely suggestions but binding decrees that establish what is right and wrong. God's authority, seen in passages like Isaiah 33:22, "*For the LORD is our judge, the LORD is our lawgiver, the LORD is our king; he will save us,"* shows that His Word stands as the final legal and moral standard.

Judgment and Reward

The Bible not only sets out the rules for righteous living but also warns of judgment and consequences for disobedience. As the formal law of God, it provides both warnings of punishment for sin and promises of reward for those who follow God's ways. Galatians 6:7 declares, "*Be not deceived; God is not mocked: for whatsoever a man soweth, that shall he also reap.*"

Resolution Through Christ

God's law, while convicting of sin, also leads to resolution and redemption through Jesus Christ. The legal framework of the Bible points to the necessity of Christ's sacrifice to fulfil the law's demands. Romans 8:1-2 states, "*There is therefore now no condemnation to them which are in Christ Jesus... For the law of the Spirit of life in Christ Jesus hath made me free from the law of sin and death.*"

2. The Bible as the Procedure of Life

God's Word provides the procedures for living a life that pleases Him. His commandments, statutes, and teachings are clear instructions on how to live. Psalm 119:9 says, "*Wherewithal shall a young man cleanse his way? by taking heed thereto according to thy word.*"

3. The Bible as the Manual of Life

Like a manual that helps us understand how things work, the Bible serves as a guide to living righteously. It teaches us how to relate to God, others, and ourselves. Proverbs 4:20-22 says, "*My son, attend to my words; incline thine ear unto my sayings... For they are life unto those that find them, and health to all their flesh.*"

The Role of God's Word in Revealing Who He Is

God's Word Reveals His Nature

God's Word is His self-revelation to humanity. Through Scripture, we come to know His holiness, love, justice, and mercy. The Bible helps us understand His character and His unchanging nature.

Christ as the Living Word

John 1:1 declares, "*In the beginning was the Word, and the Word was with God, and the Word was God.*" Jesus is the Word made flesh, the ultimate revelation of God's nature. In Christ, we see the fullness of God's character displayed.

The Power of Speaking and Declaring God's Word

Authority in the Spoken Word

When we speak God's Word in faith, it becomes a powerful tool for spiritual battles and transformation.

Isaiah 55:11 says, "*So shall my word be that goeth forth out of my mouth: it shall not return unto me void, but it shall accomplish that which I please, and it shall prosper in the thing whereto I sent it.*"

Standing on the Promises of Scripture

The Bible is full of promises that believers can stand on in faith. God's Word never fails, and when we declare His promises, we activate His power in our lives. As Matthew 24:35 reminds us, "*Heaven and earth shall pass away, but my words shall not pass away.*"

10

GOD'S ROLES

God as Creator

One of the fundamental roles of God is that of Creator. The Bible begins with the declaration of God's creative power: *"In the beginning God created the heaven and the earth"* (Genesis 1:1). This opening statement sets the stage for understanding God's sovereignty and His authority over all creation.

The Act of Creation

God's creative act is described in Genesis 1 and 2. Over six days, God creates everything from the universe to the smallest creatures. Each day of creation concludes with the phrase, "*And God saw that it was good,*" emphasising the perfection and intentionality of His work.

Humanity's Creation

The creation of humanity is distinct and special. Genesis 1:27 states, "*So God created man in His own image, in the image of God created He him; male and female created He them.*" Being made in the image of God gives humanity intrinsic value and purpose, distinguishing humans from the rest of creation. To put this in simple words, God has made humans the managers of their lives with freedom of choice.

Sustainer of Creation

God not only created the world but also sustains it. Colossians 1:17 says, "*He is before all things, and by Him all things consist.*" This sustaining role ensures the ongoing existence and order of the universe, reflecting God's continuous involvement and care.

God as Sustainer

In addition to being the Creator, God is the Sustainer of all things. His sustaining power is evident in the ongoing maintenance of the universe and the natural order.

Sustaining the Universe

Hebrews 1:3 declares, "*Who being the brightness of His glory, and the express image of His person, and upholding all things by word of His power.*" God's word upholds the universe, ensuring its stability and function.

Provision for Creation

God provides for the needs of His creation. The words of Jesus illustrate this care:

> "Look at the birds of the air; they do not sow or reap or store away in barns, and yet your heavenly Father feeds them. Are you not much more valuable than they? Can any one of you by worrying add a single hour to your life?"
>
> **Matthew 6:26-30 (NIV)**

Protection and Guidance

God's sustaining role also includes protection and guidance for His people. Psalm 121:3-4 (NIV) reassures, "*He will not let your foot slip – He who watches over you will not slumber; indeed, He who watches over Israel will neither slumber nor sleep.*" God's vigilance and care ensure the well-being of His people.

God as Redeemer

The role of God as Redeemer is central to the Christian faith. Redemption involves God's plan to save humanity from sin and restore the broken relationship between God and humans.

The Promise of Redemption

The promise of redemption is first given in Genesis 3:15, where God declares that the offspring of the woman will crush the serpent's head. This prophecy points to Jesus Christ, the ultimate Redeemer.

Jesus as the Redeemer

Jesus Christ is the fulfilment of God's redemptive plan. Through His life, death, and resurrection, Jesus provides the means for man's salvation. Ephesians 1:7 (NIV) states, "*In Him we have redemption through His blood, the forgiveness of sins, in accordance with the riches of God's grace.*"

The Work of Redemption

The work of redemption includes justification, sanctification, and glorification. Romans 5:1 explains justification: "*Therefore, since we have been justified through faith, we have peace with God through our Lord Jesus Christ.*" Sanctification is the process of becoming more like Christ, as described in 2 Corinthians 3:18. Glorification is the final transformation of believers into the likeness of Christ, as promised in Romans 8:30.

God as Judge

God's role as Judge is crucial for understanding His justice and righteousness. The Bible portrays God as the ultimate Judge who will execute justice and righteousness at the end of time.

The Basis of God's Judgment

God's judgment is based on His perfect knowledge and holiness. Ecclesiastes 12:14 (NIV) states, "*For God will bring every deed into judgment, including every hidden thing, whether it is good or evil.*" God's omniscience ensures that His judgment is fair and just.

The Day of Judgment

The New Testament emphasises the Day of Judgment, when all people will stand before God to be judged. Revelation 20:12 (NIV) describes this scene: "*And I saw the dead, great and small, standing before the Throne, and books were opened. Another book was opened, which is the Book of Life. The dead were judged according to what they had done as recorded in the Books.*"

Jesus as the Judge

Jesus Christ, who is also the Redeemer, is appointed as the Judge. God's word states:

> "Moreover, the Father judges no one, but has entrusted all judgment to the Son, that all may honor the Son just as they honor the Father. Whoever does not honor the Son does not honor the Father, who sent Him."
>
> **John 5:22-23 (NIV)**

Reflection and Application

Understanding God's roles as Creator, Sustainer, Redeemer, and Judge helps believers grasp the breadth and depth of His work in the world and in their lives. These roles illustrate God's sovereignty, care, love, and justice.

- *Worship and Adoration:* Recognise and worship God for His mighty works as Creator and Sustainer. Reflect on the beauty and order of creation, giving thanks for His continuous provision and care.

- *Trust and Dependence:* Depend on God as the Sustainer of your life. Trust in His provision and guidance, knowing that He cares for your needs and protects you.
- *Gratitude for Redemption:* Live in gratitude for God's redemptive work through Jesus Christ. Embrace the salvation offered through His sacr -ifice and commit to growing in holiness.
- *Living with Eternity in Mind:* Understand the reality of God's role as Judge and live with an eternal perspective. Strive to live righteously, knowing that your actions have eternal significance.
- *Spreading the Gospel:* Share the good news of God's redemption with others. Encourage those around you to understand and embrace the salvation available through Jesus Christ.

As we continue exploring who God is, these roles provide a framework for understanding His interactions with the world and humanity. This foundation prepares us to delve into God's works, His moral authority, and His ultimate purpose as the object of worship and devotion.

11

GOD'S WORKS

Miracles and Wonders in the Bible

The Bible is filled with examples of God's miraculous works, demonstrating His power, compassion, and involvement in the lives of His people. These miracles serve as signs of God's presence and authority, drawing attention to His ability to intervene in both natural and spiritual circumstances.

Old Testament Miracles

- *The Creation of the World:* God's first miraculous work is the creation of the heavens and the earth (Genesis 1). His omnipotence is demonstrated as He speaks all things into existence.
- *The Exodus from Egypt:* The deliverance of the Israelites from Egypt is filled with miracles, from the ten plagues to the parting of the Red Sea (Exodus 7-14).

- *Miracles through Prophets:* Prophets such as Elijah and Elisha also performed miracles, including the raising of the dead and calling down fire from heaven (1 Kings 18; 2 Kings 4).

New Testament Miracles

- *Jesus' Ministry:* Jesus performed numerous miracles—healing the sick, casting out demons, feeding the multitudes, and raising the dead (John 11:1-44; Matthew 14:13-21).
- *The Apostles:* The apostles, through the power of the Holy Spirit, continued to perform miracles, preaching the gospel with signs and wonders accompanying them (Acts 2:43).

God's Ongoing Work in the World Today

God's work did not end with the Bible. He continues to actively work in the world through the Holy Spirit. Prayers are answered, lives are changed, and His presence is evident in the lives of believers.

Answering Prayers

James 5:16 assures believers that *"the prayer of a righteous person is powerful and effective."* Through prayer, believers see God's intervention in their personal lives, in healing, provision, and guidance.

Guiding Believers

The Holy Spirit continues to guide believers into all truth, as promised in John 16:13. He directs the steps of God's people, often in ways that reveal divine intervention.

Transforming Lives

The gospel continues to change lives today. Believers around the world testify to the transformative power of knowing Christ and the difference He makes in their lives.

Personal Testimonies and Stories of God's Work

Healing and Forgiveness

In 1993, I had a deep-seated issue with my wife's brother. It worsened when my mother passed away in 1994, and he failed to offer condolences, which led me to harbour bitterness. I swore never to speak to him again, either in this life or the next. For months, I ignored him whenever I encountered him.

However, in August of 1994, after accepting Jesus Christ and becoming born-again, the LORD began to speak to me about forgiveness. This was difficult for me to accept. I argued with God, asking why I had to forgive those who had wronged me, but He persisted. One of the early ministers in my life said, "If you don't forgive, He will not forgive you." These words unsettled me, as I did not want to be estranged from the LORD, whom I had just encountered.

I asked the LORD for help, as I knew I couldn't do it on my own. Eventually, I decided to forgive, starting with a phone call to my brother-in-law. After much conversation, we reconciled. This decision set me free, giving me liberty in my spirit. Years later, when I finally met the other person I needed to forgive, a former schoolmate, I experienced complete healing in my heart. Today, both my brother-in-law and my former schoolmate are significant parts of my life, and we support each other in meaningful ways.

God's Guidance and Provision

In 2016, after spending some time in Nigeria working on family projects, I returned to the UK seeking a stable job to meet my financial needs. I prayed to the LORD for guidance, and as I researched jobs, I became interested in a position as a Supply Chain Manager. I studied the field through online resources and felt equipped to apply for the job.

One evening, while on a prayer walk, I felt the LORD guiding me to cross the road and inquire about a job posted on a billboard for Customer Delivery Drivers. Although I wasn't keen on driving, I followed His prompting and struck up a conversation with someone who encouraged me to apply. From that night on, the LORD gave me specific instructions and dreams, guiding every step of the way. I was eventually employed by the company, not as a driver but in a different role He had prepared for me.

Interestingly, when I was later shortlisted for an

interview for the supply chain position I had originally applied for, I felt no need to attend. The LORD had already led me to the place of His choosing. Though the salary wasn't what I initially hoped for, God's plan was perfect, and He provided exactly what I needed at that time.

Divine Guidance and Calling

At my current place of employment, I meet many people from diverse backgrounds. I quickly realised that many of my colleagues were spiritually destitute, with little understanding of God or the relevance of faith in their lives. Over time, God used me to witness transformations in the lives of some of these individuals as He knit us together.

It became clear to me that there was much more work to do, but I couldn't personally teach them everything I knew about God. This led me to start considering writing a book about frequently asked questions regarding God to help satisfy their hunger for truth. I took this idea to prayer during a personal retreat in August 2024, and while praying, I received clear direction from the Lord to focus on expanding the section on *Who God Is*. This was a divine confirmation of the desire in my heart and the requests from my colleagues for a simple, easy-to-read guide on understanding God.

Transformation Through the Holy Spirit

My encounter with the Holy Spirit was life-changing. Before becoming born-again, I had only heard of the Father and the Son, but the Holy Spirit was a mystery to me. After hearing a minister preach about the Holy Spirit, my curiosity grew, though I initially felt apprehensive about spiritual gifts like speaking in tongues.

I prayed for the Holy Spirit, not specifically asking for tongues, but simply for His presence. A short while later, I began to experience His overwhelming presence. One morning, as I greeted the Holy Spirit, I felt a rush of wind and a tangible presence that brought immense joy and excitement. In that moment, I received the baptism of the Holy Spirit and began speaking in tongues—a gift I had previously resisted.

From that day onward, the Holy Spirit began guiding me in profound ways. He helped me pray in difficult circumstances, warned me of impending spiritual attacks, and taught me how to hear His voice. He transformed my life, making prayer a powerful tool and giving me confidence in His presence. Through Him, I learned that I would never walk alone, and He became my constant guide in all areas of life.

Reflection and Application

Reflecting on God's works in our lives encourages us to recognise His active presence and respond with faith and gratitude. Here are practical ways to apply these principles:

1. Cultivate Gratitude

Take time to reflect on the ways God has worked in your life. Thank Him for the healing, guidance, provision, and transformation He has provided.

2. Share Your Testimony

Share your personal stories of God's work with others. Your testimony can inspire and encourage fellow believers and serve as a powerful witness to those seeking God.

3. Pray with Expectation

When you pray, do so with faith, trusting that God hears and answers. Be specific in your prayers and stay attentive to how He may be working in response.

4. Recognise God's Hand in Everyday Life

Be mindful of how God is at work in your daily life, even in the small details. Look for His guidance, provision, and protection in every situation.

5. Join in God's Work

Participate in what God is doing in your community and the world. Serve others, share the gospel, and reflect His love through your actions in all your areas of influence.

12

GOD AS THE SOURCE OF MORAL AUTHORITY AND THE ULTIMATE OBJECT OF WORSHIP AND DEVOTION

God's Moral Authority

God's moral authority is rooted in His nature and character. As the Creator and Sustainer of the universe, God establishes the moral order and defines what is right and wrong. This moral authority is revealed through His commandments, teachings, and the person of Jesus Christ.

The Basis of God's Moral Authority

God's moral authority stems from His holiness, righteousness, and omniscience. Isaiah 5:16 (NIV) states, "*But the Lord Almighty will be exalted by His justice, and the holy God will be proved holy by His righteous acts.*" God's perfect knowledge and justice ensure that His moral directives are not arbitrary but reflect His character.

The Ten Commandments

One of the clearest expressions of God's moral authority is the Ten Commandments given to Moses on Mount Sinai (Exodus 20:1-17). These commandments outline fundamental principles for living in a way that honours God and respects others. They cover aspects of worship, personal conduct, and social justice.

Jesus' Teachings

Jesus' teachings further clarify and expand upon God's moral law. In the Sermon on the Mount (Matthew 5-7), Jesus emphasises the spirit of the law, calling His followers to internalise God's commandments and live out His principles of love, mercy, and justice. Jesus summarises the moral law in His sermon:

> "'Love the LORD your God with all your heart and with all your soul and with all your mind.' This is the first and greatest commandment. And the second is like it: 'Love your neighbor as yourself.' All the Law and the Prophets hang on these two commandments."
>
> **Matthew 22:37-40**

The Importance of Worship and Devotion

Worship and devotion are central to the believer's relationship with God. They are responses to His greatness, goodness, and grace, and they align believers' hearts and lives with His purposes.

Worship in Spirit and Truth

Jesus teaches that true worshipers will worship the Father in spirit and truth (John 4:23-24). This means worshiping God with genuine hearts and minds, grounded in the truth of who He is. Worship is not merely about rituals or external actions but about an authentic relationship with God.

Expressions of Worship

Worship can be expressed in various ways, including prayer, singing, reading Scripture, and acts of service. The Psalms, for example, are filled with songs and prayers that express praise, thanksgiving, lament, and supplication. Worship involves acknow-ledging God's worthiness and exalting Him above all else.

Devotion Through Obedience

True devotion to God is demonstrated through obedience to His commandments. Jesus said, "*If you love me, keep my commands*" (John 14:15). Obedience is an act of worship that reflects a heart committed to God's will. It involves aligning one's actions, thoughts, and desires with God's principles.

Practical Ways to Live Out Worship and Devotion

1. Daily Prayer and Meditation

Spend time each day in prayer and meditation, focusing on God's attributes, thanking Him for His blessings, and seeking His guidance.

2. Scripture Reading and Study

Regularly read and study the Bible to understand God's character, His moral law, and His promises. Allow His Word to shape your beliefs and actions.

3. Corporate Worship

Participate in corporate worship with other believers. Gatherings for worship, such as church services, provide opportunities to collectively praise God, hear His Word, and encourage one another.

4. Acts of Service

Serve others as an expression of your love for God. Jesus taught that serving others is a form of worship (Matthew 25:40). Look for ways to help those in need, showing God's love through your actions.

5. Cultivate a Heart of Gratitude

Develop an attitude of gratitude by regularly reflecting on God's goodness and blessings. Thankfulness is a key aspect of worship and keeps your focus on God's faithfulness.

6. Live a Holy Life

Strive to live a life that reflects God's holiness. Avoid actions and attitudes that are contrary to His nature. Seek His help to grow in righteousness and purity.

God as the Ultimate Object of Worship and Devotion

God alone is worthy of worship and devotion. He is the Creator, Sustainer, Redeemer, and Judge of all things. As believers, our ultimate purpose is to glorify God and enjoy a relationship with Him.

Worship in Eternity

The book of Revelation gives a glimpse of eternal worship in heaven. Revelation 4:11 (NIV) records the praise of the heavenly beings: "*You are worthy, our LORD and God, to receive glory and honor and power, for You created all things, and by Your will they were created and have their being.*" This eternal worship reflects the continuous acknowledgment of God's supremacy and majesty.

Devotion as a Way of Life

Devotion to God is not limited to specific times or places; it is a way of life. Colossians 3:17 (NIV) instructs, "*And whatever you do, whether in word or deed, do it all in the name of the LORD Jesus, giving thanks to God the Father through Him.*" Every aspect of a believer's life can be an act of worship when done with a heart devoted to God.

Reflection and Application

Reflecting on God as the source of moral authority and the ultimate object of worship and devotion challenges believers to examine their lives and align themselves with His will. Here are practical steps to apply these principles:

1. *Evaluate Your Priorities*

Assess what holds the highest place in your life. Ensure that God is your ultimate priority, above all other pursuits and desires.

2. *Cultivate a Lifestyle of Worship*

Integrate worship into your daily routine. Use moments throughout the day to praise God, reflect on His goodness, and seek His presence.

3. *Embrace God's Moral Authority*

Align your moral values and decisions with God's Word. Seek to live out His commandments in every area of your life.

4. *Engage in Continuous Learning*

Commit to growing in your understanding of God's nature and His ways. Attend Bible studies, read theological books, and engage in discussions with other believers.

5. *Practice Humility and Reverence*

Approach God with humility and reverence, recognising His greatness and your dependence on

Him. Let this attitude shape your interactions with others.

As we conclude this exploration of who God is, recognising His moral authority and our call to worship and devotion leads us to a deeper, more fulfilling relationship with Him. This understanding also prepares us to explore God's glory and manifestations, and His role as the Judge of the Universe.

13

GOD'S GLORY AND MANIFESTATIONS

The concept of God's glory is a central theme in the Bible, representing His majestic presence, divine splendour, and supreme authority. God's glory is manifested in various ways throughout Scripture, providing profound insights into His nature and character.

The Glory of God in the Old Testament

1. Theophanies

These are appearances of God in a tangible form. One notable example is the burning bush encounter between God and Moses. In Exodus 3:2-4, God's glory is revealed through the burning bush that is not consumed by fire. This manifestation demonstrates God's holy presence and His call to Moses to deliver the Israelites from Egypt.

2. Mount Sinai

When God gave the Ten Commandments to Moses on Mount Sinai, His glory was displayed in a dramatic way. Exodus 24:16-17 (NIV) describes the scene: "*And the glory of the LORD settled on Mount Sinai. For six days the cloud covered the mountain, and on the seventh day the Lord called to Moses from within the cloud. To the Israelites the glory of the LORD looked like a consuming fire on top of the mountain.*"

3. The Tabernacle and Temple

God's glory filled the Tabernacle and later the Temple, signifying His dwelling among His people. Exodus 40:34-35 (NIV) recounts the moment God's glory filled the Tabernacle: "*Then the cloud covered the tent of meeting, and the glory of the LORD filled the tabernacle. Moses could not enter the tent of meeting because the cloud had settled on it, and the glory of the LORD filled the tabernacle.*"

The Glory of God in the New Testament

1. The Incarnation

The incarnation of Jesus Christ is the ultimate manifestation of God's glory. John 1:14 (NIV) declares, "*The Word became flesh and made His dwelling among us. We have seen His glory, the glory of the one and only Son, who came from the Father, full of grace and truth.*" Jesus' life, teachings, miracles, death, and resurrection all reveal God's glory.

2. The Transfiguration

During the transfiguration of Jesus, His divine glory was revealed to Peter, James, and John. Matthew 17:2,3,5 describes the event: "*And was transfigured before them and His face did shine as the sun, and His raiment was white as the light. And, behold, there appeared unto them Moses and Elias talking with Him... a bright cloud overshadowed them: and behold a voice out of the cloud, which said THIS IS MY BELOVED SON, IN WHOM I AM WELL PLEASED; HEAR YE HIM.*" This moment affirmed Jesus' divine nature and His fulfilment of the Law and the Prophets.

3. Pentecost

The coming of the Holy Spirit at Pentecost was marked by a powerful manifestation of God's glory. Acts 2:2-4 recounts, "*And suddenly there came a sound from heaven as of a rushing mighty wind, and it filled the house where they were sitting. And there appeared unto them cloven tongues as of fire, and it sat upon each of them. And they were all filled with the Holy Ghost and began to speak with other tongues, as the Spirit gave them utterance.*"

The Significance of God's Glory for Believers

God's glory has profound implications for believers. It reveals His majesty, inspires worship, and transforms lives.

1. Revelation of God's Nature

God's glory reveals His holiness, power, and love. By contemplating His glory, believers gain a deeper understanding of who God is and how He relates to His creation.

2. Inspiration for Worship

Experiencing or reflecting on God's glory naturally leads to worship. Isaiah's vision of God's glory in Isaiah 6:1-4 elicited a response of awe and reverence, as the Seraphims declared, "*Holy, Holy, Holy is the LORD of Hosts; the whole earth is full of His glory.*"

3. Transformation

Contemplating God's glory transforms believers into His likeness. 2 Corinthians 3:18 explains, "*But we all, with open face beholding as in a glass the glory of the LORD, are changed into the same image from glory to glory, even as by the Spirit of the LORD.*" This transformation involves growing in holiness, love, and obedience to God.

4. Hope and Assurance

God's glory provides hope and assurance for believers. The promise of sharing in God's glory in the future motivates believers to persevere in faith. Romans 8:18 states, "*For I reckon that the sufferings of this present time are not worthy to be compared with the glory which shall be revealed in us.*"

How God's Glory is Manifested Today

1. Through Creation

God's glory is evident in the beauty and complexity of creation. Psalm 19:1 proclaims, "*The heavens declare the glory of God; the firmament sheweth His handywork.*" Observing nature can lead believers to worship and marvel at God's creativity and power.

2. In the Church

God's glory is manifested in the life of the church. Ephesians 3:21 says, "*Unto Him be glory in the church by Christ Jesus throughout all ages, world without end. Amen.*" The unity, love, and service of the church reflect God's glory to the world.

3. In the Lives of Believers

Believers are called to reflect God's glory in their daily lives. Matthew 5:16 encourages, "*Let your light so shine before men, that they may see your good works and glorify your Father which is in heaven.*" Acts of kindness, love, and faithfulness demonstrate God's presence and character.

Reflection and Application

Reflecting on God's glory encourages believers to live in a way that honours Him and displays His character to the world. Here are practical steps to apply these principles:

1. Contemplate God's Glory

Spend time in prayer and meditation, reflecting on the instances of God's glory revealed in Scripture and creation.

2. Engage in Worship

Make worship a regular part of your life, both individually and corporately. Worship God for His majesty, power, and love.

3. Pursue Holiness

Allow the contemplation of God's glory to transform your character. Strive to grow in holiness, aligning your life with God's standards.

4. Share God's Glory

Reflect God's glory to others through your actions and words. Be a witness to His goodness and grace in your interactions with others.

5. Find Hope in God's Glory

In times of difficulty, remember the promise of sharing in God's glory. Let this hope provide strength and encouragement to persevere in faith.

As we continue exploring who God is, understanding His glory and manifestations deepens our appreciation of His majesty and draws us closer to Him. This foundation prepares us to explore God's role as the Judge of the Universe.

14

GOD AS THE JUDGE OF THE UNIVERSE

God's role as the Judge of the universe is a central theme throughout Scripture. His judgment is an expression of His holiness, righteousness, and justice. Understanding God as Judge provides a comprehensive view of His character and His ultimate authority over all creation.

God's Judgment in the Old Testament

In the Old Testament, God's judgment is often portrayed in response to sin and disobedience. Some notable examples include:

1. The Flood

In Genesis 6-9, God judges the wickedness of humanity with a global flood, sparing only Noah and his family. This event underscores God's intolerance of sin and His commitment to righteousness.

2. *Sodom and Gomorrah*

In Genesis 18-19, God judges the cities of Sodom and Gomorrah for their grave sin, destroying them with fire and brimstone. This judgment serves as a warning against pervasive wickedness.

3. *The Plagues of Egypt*

In Exodus 7-12, God sends ten plagues upon Egypt to compel Pharaoh to release the Israelites from slavery. These plagues demonstrate God's power and justice in liberating His people.

God's Judgment in the New Testament

The New Testament continues the theme of God's judgment, emphasising both present and future aspects.

1. *The Ministry of Jesus*

Jesus spoke frequently about judgment, highlighting the need for repentance and faith. In Matthew 25:31-46, Jesus describes the final judgment, where the righteous are rewarded and the wicked are condemnned based on their actions.

2. *The Apostolic Teachings*

The apostles taught about God's judgment, warning believers to live righteously. Paul, in Romans 2:6-8, explains, "*Who will render to every man according to his deeds: To them who by patient continuance in well doing seek for glory and honour and immortality, eternal life: But unto them that are contentious, and do not obey the truth, but obey unrighteousness, indignation and wrath."*

3. The Book of Revelation

Revelation provides a vivid picture of the final judgment. Revelation 20:11-15 describes the Great White Throne Judgment, where the dead are judged according to their deeds and those not found in the book of life are cast into the lake of fire.

The Final Judgment and Its Implications

The final judgment is a pivotal event in Christian eschatology. It underscores the ultimate account-ability of every individual to God and the eternal consequences of their choices.

1. The Criteria of Judgment

The Bible teaches that individuals will be judged based on their actions and their relationship with God. Jesus emphasised that even our words and thoughts will be subject to judgment (Matthew 12:36-37).

2. The Role of Jesus as Judge

Jesus Christ, who is both Savior and Judge, will preside over the final judgment. John 5:22-23 states, "*For the Father judgeth no man, but hath committed all judgment unto the Son: That all men should honour the Son, even as they honour the Father."*

3. The Outcomes of Judgment

The final judgment will result in eternal life for the righteous and eternal separation from God for the wicked. Matthew 25:46 summarises, "*And these shall go away into everlasting punishment: But the righteous into life eternal.*"

Living in Light of God's Judgment

Understanding God as Judge influences how believers live their lives. It instils a sense of accountability, encourages righteous living, and fosters hope in God's ultimate justice.

1. Accountability

Knowing that we will stand before God as Judge motivates believers to live responsibly. Hebrews 4:13 reminds us, "*Neither is there any creature that is not manifest in His sight: but all things are naked and opened unto the eyes of Him with whom we have to do.*"

2. Righteous Living

Believers are called to pursue righteousness and avoid sin. 1 Peter 1:17 instructs, "*And if ye call on the Father, who without respect of persons judgeth according to every man's work, pass the time of your sojourning here in fear.*"

3. Hope and Justice

The promise of God's judgment assures believers that justice will ultimately prevail. God's word offers hope:

> "And God shall wipe away all tears from their eyes and there shall be no more death, neither sorrow, nor crying, neither shall there be any more pain: for the former things are passed away. "And He that sat upon the throne said Behold, I make all things new. And He said unto me, write for these words are true and faithful."
>
> **Revelation 21:4-5**

Reflection and Application

Reflecting on God as the Judge of the universe encourages believers to live with an eternal perspective and a commitment to righteousness. Here are some practical steps that will help with the application of these principles:

1. Examine Your Life

Regularly assess your actions, thoughts, and motivations in light of God's standards. Seek to align your life with His will.

2. Repent and Seek Forgiveness

Confess your sins and seek God's forgiveness through Jesus Christ. 1 John 1:9 assures, "*If we confess our sins, He is faithful and just to forgive us our sins, and to cleanse us from all unrighteousness.*"

3. *Live with Integrity*

Strive to live a life of integrity, knowing that God sees and knows everything. Let your actions reflect your faith and commitment to God.

4. *Encourage Others*

Share the message of God's judgment and the hope of salvation with others. Encourage them to turn to God and live righteously.

5. *Trust in God's Justice*

When faced with injustice or suffering, trust that God will ultimately bring about justice. Let this assurance provide comfort and strength.

* * *

As we conclude this exploration of who God is, recognising Him as the Judge of the universe underscores His sovereignty, justice, and the eternal significance of our choices. This understanding enriches our relationship with God and motivates us to live in a way that honours Him.

CONCLUSION

Understanding who God is forms the foundation of a meaningful and transformative relationship with Him. Through this exploration, we have delved into various aspects of God's nature, roles, and works, gaining a deeper appreciation of His majesty, love, and justice.

Recap of Key Points

1. God in Eternity Past

We began by contemplating God's eternal existence, His timeless nature, and the significance of His eternal presence for believers. Understanding that God has always been and always will be provides a sense of security and trust in His unchanging character.

2. God Proving His Subjects

We explored how God tested and refined His people throughout history, using trials to reveal and strengthen their faith. These tests serve as reminders of God's sovereignty and His desire to develop our character and trust in Him.

3. The Power and Authority of God's Word

God's Word is both the written law and the spoken truth, forming the foundation of our knowledge of Him. It serves as a formal authority, life manual, and binding decree, revealing God's will and instructing us in His ways.

4. The Name of God

We explored the significance of God's names—like Jehovah Jireh and Jehovah Rapha—which reveal His character as our Provider, Healer, and Protector. His names invite us to call upon Him in times of need.

5. God's Personal Account of Creation and the Fall of Man

The creation narrative and the fall of man highlight God's creative power and the consequences of sin. Understanding the origins of humanity's broken relationship with God sets the stage for appreciating His redemptive plan.

6. God's Plan for Humanity - Through Jesus

Central to God's plan for humanity is the life, death, and resurrection of Jesus Christ. Jesus' sacrificial love and atoning work provide the means for reconciliation with God, forgiveness of sins, and the promise of eternal life.

7. God as a Father

We examined the comforting and nurturing aspects of God's fatherhood. His love, provision, discipline, and guidance underscore the intimacy and care He extends to His children.

8. The Holy Spirit, Nature, and Divine Attributes

The role of the Holy Spirit in the believer's life and God's divine attributes—omniscience, omnipotence, omnipresence, immutability, holiness, love, and justice—reveal the depth and breadth of God's character and His active involvement in our lives. The Holy Spirit empowers and leads us in understanding God more deeply.

9. God's Roles

God's multifaceted roles as Creator, Sustainer, Redeemer, and Judge highlight His comprehensive authority and care over creation and humanity. Each role underscores a different aspect of His relationship with us.

10. God's Works

From miracles and wonders in the Bible to His ongoing work in the world today, God's actions demonstrate His power, compassion, and presence. Personal testimonies and biblical accounts illustrate His faithfulness and transformative impact.

11. God as the Source of Moral Authority and the Ultimate Object of Worship and Devotion

God's moral authority, expressed through His commandments and teachings, guides believers in righteous living. Worship and devotion are responses to His greatness and goodness, aligning our hearts and lives with His purposes.

12. God's Glory and Manifestations

The manifestations of God's glory in the Bible and today reveal His majestic presence and inspire worship. Contemplating His glory transforms believers and provides hope and assurance of sharing in His glory (1 John 3:2).

13. God as the Judge of the Universe

Understanding God as the ultimate Judge emphasises His justice, righteousness, and the eternal significance of our choices. This perspective encourages accountability, righteous living, and trust in His ultimate justice. As the righteous Judge, God holds all of creation accountable, assuring us that justice will ultimately prevail.

Encouragement for Further Study and Growth

This book serves as a starting point, offering a foundational understanding of God for a deeper exploration of who God is. Continue to seek Him through His Word, prayer, and fellowship, allowing the Holy Spirit to guide you in your journey.

The following steps are also helpful:

1. *Engage with Scripture*

Regularly read and study the Bible to learn more about God's character, promises, and teachings. Let His Word shape your beliefs and actions.

2. *Participate in Worship and Fellowship*

Join a community of believers for worship, study, and mutual encouragement. Corporate worship and fellowship provide support and opportunities for growth.

3. *Pray Continually*

Develop a habit and lifestyle of continuous prayer, seeking God's presence, guidance, and wisdom in every aspect of your life.

4. Serve Others

Reflect God's love by serving those in need. Acts of kindness and service are powerful expressions of your faith and devotion.

5. Reflect on God's Attributes

Meditate on God's attributes and how they influence your understanding of Him. Contemplating His holiness, love, justice, and other attributes deepens your appreciation and worship.

Final Thoughts

Knowing God is the key to understanding life itself. His eternal nature, redemptive plan through Jesus, fatherly care, and righteous judgment provides a comprehensive picture of His relationship with humanity. As you continue your journey of faith, may this knowledge inspire you to live a life that honours God and reflects His love and grace to the world.

May you grow in the grace and knowledge of our LORD and Savior, Jesus Christ. To Him be the glory, both now and forever. Amen.

About the Author

Olabode Winsala's quest for God began at an early age, sparked by difficult and traumatic experiences during Nigeria's political upheavals in the 1960s. As a young child between the ages of 7 and 8, Olabode witnessed the horrors of Operation Wet-e, a period marked by violence, fear, and destruction as mobs maimed, killed, and burned properties. Having previously witnessed a neighbour's tragic death in an accident and the loss of close family members, this period left him with deep questions about life and death: "What is life about? Why are we here? What happens when people die? Will we ever see them again? Who is God, and where exactly is He?"

These questions ignited a lifelong journey to understand God's nature and His plan for humanity, a journey that continues to drive Olabode's passion for sharing Biblical truth with others. Over the years, through his involvement in ministries like *The Men's*

Calvary, *Men Arise*, and *The Disciples*, Olabode has helped others confront their own questions about God and life, providing guidance and teaching that leads to a deeper relationship with God.

As a member of *Lea Valley Church* in Waltham Abbey, UK, Olabode remains an active part of his local Christian community. He holds a B.Sc. in Sociology and a Master's in Industrial and Labour Relations from the University of Ibadan, Nigeria. Combining his academic background with a passion for people, Olabode shares insights that bridge Biblical wisdom with practical living.

In addition to his ministry work, Olabode is launching a blog titled "Personal With God," along with a corresponding YouTube channel, where he will dive deeper into the themes explored in this book and share reflections on walking with God in everyday life.

When not writing or engaging in ministry, Olabode enjoys watching football, athletics, films and taking "prayer walks," which he fondly refers to as his personal "walk with God." He lives in the United Kingdom with his family, where they continue to seek God's will together.

Printed in Great Britain
by Amazon

59416311R00066